PAPER PEONY PRESS

A MOTHER DAUGHTER JOURNAL
BY CASEY-LEIGH WIEGAND

Thanks so much for buying our book!
For a free extra, email

paperpeonypress@gmail.com

and we will send something
fun to your inbox!

Heart to Heart: A Mother Daughter Journal
© Casey Leigh Wiegand
First Edition, 2023

Published by: Paper Peony Press
@paperpeonypress
www.paperpeonypress.com

All rights reserved. *Heart to Heart: A Mother Daughter Journal* is under copyright protection. No part of this journal may be used or reproduced in any manner whatsoever without written permission except in the case of brief quotations embodied in critical articles and reviews.

For wholesale inquiries contact: reagan@paperpeonypress.com

Illustration © Casey Leigh Wiegand

Copy-writing © Brhea Koneman

Lettering © Skyler Villarreal

Printed in China

978-1-961355-00-2

This journal is dedicated to my precious girls. Being your mama is the most beautiful gift in the world. Girls, what you speak over yourselves, the words that you share when talking to others matter! Shine your lights ! Getting to truly see you, KNOW you and hear your heart is a treasure I'll never get over- this journal is a piece of sharing what we have together with the world! I love you!

HOW TO USE THIS JOURNAL

This journal is about you and your unique story. I created this journal to fit within the pages of your life.

Whether you decide to make this journal part of your weekly routine, or you choose special occasions to sit together to fill out its pages — your story is recorded in the beautiful way that could only be authentically yours.

I hope that this journal prompts you to take intentional time as mother and daughter. When filling out its pages, it is my dream that you feel the true importance of your own story, and take note of the many gifts in your life.

You will find mother/daughter/together flags like the ones below throughout the book to indicate who fills out each page.

Think of ways that you can prompt the use of this journal, maybe leave it out with a pencil on the desk in your daughter's room, or grab it and bring it into her room during your bedtime routine. Sweet moments like this are created with intentionality.

Encourage your daughter to leave the journal for you to read or for you to fill out too. This can be a love letter of sorts between the two of you, left out on a night stand, or packed into a travel bag for a trip — a special gesture to remind one another of the importance of your relationship and connection.

My prayer is that these pages are filled out over time, and that in writing to one another you are able to express yourselves, and to better know one another.

When I share my heart,
I remember that her
eyes are watching.
May she always know
that her story matters,
she is a gift + a light.

Mother Daughter Day Ideas

When you need some inspiration for a fun activity together, look through this list, choose and enjoy! Be sure to check it off when you're done!

- ☐ Mani-Pedis
- ☐ Double Feature Movie Night
- ☐ Baking Day
- ☐ Bike Ride
- ☐ Roller Rink
- ☐ Mall Day
- ☐ Library
- ☐ Art Class
- ☐ Concert
- ☐ Fancy Dinner Out
- ☐ Breakfast Date
- ☐ Hike
- ☐ Pool/Beach/Lake Day
- ☐ Museum
- ☐ Volunteer in Our Community
- ☐ Nature Walk
- ☐ Road Trip

Our Bucket List

Take time to brainstorm a list of the top 10 things you hope to accomplish together!

1. _____

2. _____

3. _____

4. _____

5. _____

6. _____

7. _____

8. _____

9. _____

10. _____

CONVERSATION STARTERS

Use these questions as a way to spark conversations at different times of the day. You will never regret building a habit of talking together, whether on a drive, during dinnertime or at bedtime!

- If we could have a mother-daughter day just us two, how would you want to spend the entire day?

- What is something about you that you wish others noticed more?

- Is there anything that you wish we talked more about or that you long to share with me?

- What is a skill or ability that you want to learn how to do / practice more?

- What are some things that you think we have in common?

- What are some parts of you that you feel are unique or different from me?

I love it when you...

Poop

I wish we did more of...

I love it when you...

_____
_____
_____
_____
_____
_____
_____
_____
_____
_____

I wish we did more of..

_____
_____
_____
_____
_____
_____
_____
_____
_____
_____

Daughter

ask me anything

Something I want to ask you today, daughter...

Q:
_____
_____
_____
_____
_____
_____
_____

A:
_____
_____
_____
_____
_____
_____
_____

Mother

ask me anything

Something I want to ask you today, Mom...

Q:

A:

Daughter

Dear Daughter,

Mother

Dear Mom,

Daughter

List it out!

5 THINGS I LOVE ABOUT MY DAUGHTER...

1.

2.

3.

4.

5.

Mother

List it out!

5 THINGS I LOVE ABOUT MY MOM...

1.

2.

3.

4.

5.

Daughter

I HOPE THAT MY TRUEST SELF
BRINGS OUT HER TRUEST SELF.
DIFFERENT, YET THE SAME AT HEART.
MOTHER AND DAUGHTER
TOGETHER A WORK OF ART.

Dear Mom,

Daughter

this or that

---- *circle your preference* ----

INSIDE	OUTSIDE
ART	SPORTS
READING	WRITING
VACATION	STAY-CATION
FUNNY MOVIE	SCARY MOVIE
BOAT DAY	POOL DAY
COOK AT HOME	EAT AT RESTAURANT
TIME ALONE	TIME WITH FRIENDS
TIDY	MESSY
ON TIME	RUNNING LATE
EXTROVERTED	INTROVERTED
SUNSHINEY	MELANCHOLY
SNEAKERS	FANCY SHOES
TEAM SPORTS	SOLO SPORTS

Mother

this or that

— circle your preference —

INSIDE / OUTSIDE

ART / SPORTS

READING / WRITING

VACATION / STAY-CATION

FUNNY MOVIE / SCARY MOVIE

BOAT DAY / POOL DAY

COOK AT HOME / EAT AT RESTAURANT

TIME ALONE / TIME WITH FRIENDS

TIDY / MESSY

ON TIME / RUNNING LATE

EXTROVERTED / INTROVERTED

SUNSHINEY / MELANCHOLY

SNEAKERS / FANCY SHOES

TEAM SPORTS / SOLO SPORTS

Daughter

Something I admire about you is..

When I look at you I see...

Mother

Something I admire about you is..

When I look at you I see...

Daughter

My Favorites

ENTERTAINMENT EDITION

MOVIE _____

TV SHOW _____

ACTOR/ACTRESS _____

BOOK _____

AUTHOR _____

LITERARY GENRE _____

SONG _____

SINGER _____

BEST CONCERT EVER _____

Mother

My Favorites

ENTERTAINMENT EDITION

MOVIE _____

TV SHOW _____

ACTOR/ACTRESS _____

BOOK _____

AUTHOR _____

LITERARY GENRE _____

SONG _____

SINGER _____

BEST CONCERT EVER _____

Daughter

Dear Daughter,

Mother

Dear Mom,

Daughter

Dear Daughter,

Mother

Precious Daughter, Watching you grow into who you are meant to be is the greatest blessing. I am proud of all that you are becoming each day, always & in every way.

When you are overwhelmed, I would encourage you to...

_____
_____
_____
_____
_____
_____
_____
_____
_____
_____
_____

I hope you always know...

_____
_____
_____
_____
_____
_____
_____
_____
_____
_____
_____

Mother

When I am overwhelmed, it's the most helpful when you...

_____
_____
_____
_____
_____
_____
_____
_____
_____
_____

I hope you always know...

_____
_____
_____
_____
_____
_____
_____
_____
_____
_____

Daughter

I see you Daughter...

and all of the things that make you, you.
I love that you…

_____

_____

_____

_____

_____

_____

_____

_____

_____

Dear Mom,

Daughter

Let's Dream Together

AS YOU GROW UP...

- I think you'll be _____ (career).

- I think you'll have _____ kids.

- I think you'll live in _____ (city).

- Something that I think will always remain about you
  _____.

- I hope that you spend your time doing lots of
  _____.

- I think your favorite hobby will be
  _____.

- I think your favorite meal will be
  _____.

- I think the type of house that you live in will be
  _____.

- I think our favorite thing to do together will be
  _____.

Mother

AS I GROW UP...

- I want to be a _____ when I grow up.

- I want to have _____ kids.

- I want to live in _____ (city).

- Something that I think will always remain within me
_____.

- I hope that I do lots of
_____.

- I think my favorite hobby will be
_____.

- I think my favorite meal will be
_____.

- I think the type of house that I live in will be
_____.

- I think our favorite thing to do together will be
_____.

Daughter

Dear Daughter,

Mother

Dear Mom,

Daughter

ask me anything

Something I want to ask you today, daughter...

Q:

A:

Mother

ask me anything

Something I want to ask you today, Mom...

Q:

A:

Daughter

To know you is to love you,
my sweet girl.
I've longed for you since
before your birth.
Let's write our stories
together,
while they overlap
here on earth.

Dear Mom,

Daughter

My favorite thing about my daughter is…

_____
_____
_____
_____
_____
_____
_____

My favorite thing about being a mother is…

_____
_____
_____
_____
_____
_____
_____

My favorite thing we have in common is…

_____
_____
_____
_____
_____
_____
_____

Mother

My favorite thing about my mom is…

My favorite thing about me is…

My favorite thing we have in common is…

Daughter

My Favorites

REMEMBERING MOM'S SCHOOL DAYS EDITION

SCHOOL LUNCH: _____

EXTRACURRICULAR ACTIVITY: _____

YEAR OR GRADE: _____

SPORT: _____

TEACHER: _____

SCHOOL CELEBRATION: _____

BOOK I READ IN SCHOOL: _____

INSTRUMENT OR STYLE OF MUSIC: _____

TYPE OF ART TO CREATE: _____

Mother

My Favorites

SCHOOL EDITION

SCHOOL LUNCH: _____

EXTRACURRICULAR ACTIVITY: _____

YEAR OR GRADE: _____

SPORT: _____

TEACHER: _____

SCHOOL CELEBRATION: _____

BOOK I'VE READ IN SCHOOL: _____

INSTRUMENT OR STYLE OF MUSIC: _____

TYPE OF ART TO CREATE: _____

Daughter

Dear Mom,

Daughter

List it out!

5 PLACES WE WANT TO VISIT TOGETHER:

1.

2.

3.

4.

5.

Together

place photo here

Dear Daughter,

Mother

Just as I've carried you
with me, first in my heart,
next in my arms;
then your hand
in mine

you will carry
my love with you

Forevermore

Let's Dream Together

TELL ME ABOUT YOUR DREAM HOME...

- What color will your kitchen be?

  _____

- How many bedrooms do you want? _____
- Will your home be traditional or modern?

  _____

- What colors will you decorate with?

  _____

- What is something unique about your house?

  _____

- What are three words that describe how you want to feel in your home?

  _____

  _____

  _____

- Will you like to have lots of people over, or to have a more quiet home?

  _____

Daughter

● Draw a picture of your future home...

Daughter

How do you most like to receive love from me?

How do you most like to give love to others?

How do you most like to receive love from me?

How do you most like to give love to others?

Daughter

Trace your hand!

Mother

Trace your hand!

Daughter

Dear Daughter,

Mother

Dear Mom,

Daughter

My Favorites

TRAVEL EDITION

DESTINATION: _____

WEATHER: _____

HOTEL WE'VE STAYED AT: _____

THING TO DO ON VACATION: _____

MOST BEAUTIFUL PLACE WE'VE SEEN: _____

MOST UNEXPECTED TRIP WE'VE TAKEN: _____

PLACE TO RETURN TO YEAR AFTER YEAR: _____

RELAXING ACTIVITY: _____

PLACE WHERE MY SOUL COMES ALIVE: _____

Mother

My Favorites

TRAVEL EDITION

DESTINATION: _____

WEATHER: _____

HOTEL WE'VE STAYED AT: _____

THING TO DO ON VACATION: _____

MOST BEAUTIFUL PLACE WE'VE SEEN: _____

MOST UNEXPECTED TRIP WE'VE TAKEN: _____

PLACE TO RETURN TO YEAR AFTER YEAR: _____

RELAXING ACTIVITY: _____

PLACE WHERE MY SOUL COMES ALIVE: _____

Daughter

Daughter,
you radiate beauty and kindness. Time spent with you is a treasure. I hope that you always hold onto who you are.

Dear Mom,

Daughter

Tell me about a favorite memory from your childhood.

How did you feel in that moment?

Mother

Tell me about a favorite memory from your childhood.

___

How did you feel in that moment?

___

Daughter

ask me anything

Something I want to ask you today, daughter...

Q: _____
_____
_____
_____
_____
_____

A: _____
_____
_____
_____
_____
_____

Mother

ask me anything

Something I want to ask you today, Mom...

Q:

A:

Daughter

Dear Daughter,

Mother

this or that

— *circle your preference* —

ICE CREAM	CAKE
MOVIE	TV SHOW
DANCE	SING
QUIET NIGHT IN	FAMILY FUN NIGHT OUT
CARNIVAL	THEME PARK
CATS	DOGS
RAINY DAY	SUNNY DAY
SPICY FOOD	SWEET FOOD
HIKE	BIKE RIDE
ROLLER SKATING	ICE SKATING
QUIET TIME	PARTY TIME
WINTER	SUMMER
FALL	SPRING
BEACH	MOUNTAINS

Mother

this or that

———— circle your preference ————

ICE CREAM | CAKE

MOVIE | TV SHOW

DANCE | SING

QUIET NIGHT IN | FAMILY FUN NIGHT OUT

CARNIVAL | THEME PARK

CATS | DOGS

RAINY DAY | SUNNY DAY

SPICY FOOD | SWEET FOOD

HIKE | BIKE RIDE

ROLLER SKATING | ICE SKATING

QUIET TIME | PARTY TIME

WINTER | SUMMER

FALL | SPRING

BEACH | MOUNTAINS

Daughter

Dear Daughter,

Mother

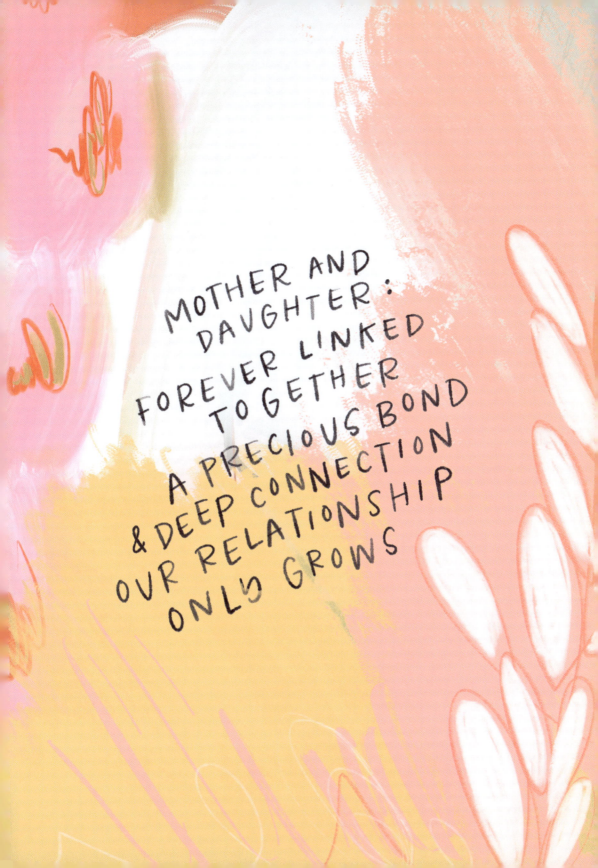

Mother and daughter:
forever linked
together
a precious bond
& deep connection
our relationship
only grows

Tell me about something that you daydream about.

_____

Why do you think this is a dream of yours?

_____

Mother

Tell me about something that you daydream about.

_____
_____
_____
_____
_____
_____
_____
_____
_____
_____

Why do you think this is a dream of yours?

_____
_____
_____
_____
_____
_____
_____
_____
_____
_____

Daughter

My Favorites

FOOD EDITION

MEAL: _____

SWEET TREAT: _____

RESTAURANT: _____

SNACK: _____

THING TO COOK: _____

HOLIDAY MEAL: _____

FAMILY RECIPE: _____

MOM'S SPECIALTY: _____

COMFORT FOOD: _____

Mother

My Favorites

FOOD EDITION

MEAL: _____

SWEET TREAT: _____

RESTAURANT: _____

SNACK: _____

THING TO COOK: _____

HOLIDAY MEAL: _____

FAMILY RECIPE: _____

MOM'S SPECIALTY: _____

COMFORT FOOD: _____

Daughter

this or that

— circle your preference —

SOMEPLACE WARM	SOMEPLACE COLD
BY THE WATER	MOSTLY LAND
COUNTRY	CITY
OVERSEAS	HOME COUNTRY
PLANE	ROAD TRIP
HOTEL	HOME RENTAL
SHORT TRIP	LONG TRIP
MEALS OUT	KITCHEN TO COOK IN
SIGHTSEEING	STAY MOSTLY AT LOCATION
FAST PACED	SLOW AND RELAXING
PLANNED OUT AHEAD	SPONTANEOUS TRIP
LOTS OF FREE TIME	LOTS OF ACTIVITIES SCHEDULED
MULTIPLE CITIES	ONE DESTINATION

Mother

this or that

circle your preference

SOMEPLACE WARM	SOMEPLACE COLD
BY THE WATER	MOSTLY LAND
COUNTRY	CITY
OVERSEAS	HOME COUNTRY
PLANE	ROAD TRIP
HOTEL	HOME RENTAL
SHORT TRIP	LONG TRIP
MEALS OUT	KITCHEN TO COOK IN
SIGHTSEEING	STAY MOSTLY AT LOCATION
FAST PACED	SLOW AND RELAXING
PLANNED OUT AHEAD	SPONTANEOUS TRIP
LOTS OF FREE TIME	LOTS OF ACTIVITIES SCHEDULED
MULTIPLE CITIES	ONE DESTINATION

Daughter

Dear Daughter,

Mother

Dear Mom,

Daughter

List it out!

10 THINGS WE LOVE ABOUT OUR FAMILY:

1.
2.
3.
4.
5.
6.
7.
8.
9.
10.

Together

Mama, your best is more than enough. All that you pour in matters. I hope that you always know how loved you are.

Dear Mom,

Daughter

If you could have one wish granted, what would it be?

How do you think life might change if you got this wish?

Mother

If you could have one wish granted, what would it be?

How do you think life might change if you got this wish?

Daughter

Dear Daughter,

Mother

I see you Mama...

and all of the many things you do for me each day.
I notice how you...

_____

_____

_____

_____

_____

_____

_____

_____

_____

_____

Dear Daughter,

Mother

Dear Mom,

Daughter

ask me anything

Something I want to ask you today, daughter...

Q:

A:

Mother

ask me anything

Something I want to ask you today, Mom...

Q:

A:

Daughter

Dear Daughter,

Mother

Tell me about something that you are interested in that I might not know about...

Mother

Tell me about something that you are interested in that I might not know about...

Daughter

this or that

— circle your preference —

FANCY	SIMPLE
PAINTED NAILS	NATURAL NAILS
HAIRSTYLE	NATURAL HAIR
DRESSY OUTFIT	COZY JAMMIES
DRESS SHOES	SNEAKERS
DRESS	PANTS
MAKEUP	FRESH FACE
JEWELRY	NO JEWELRY
WARM WEATHER CLOTHES	COLD WEATHER CLOTHES
BRIGHT COLORS	NEUTRALS
NO UNIFORM	SCHOOL UNIFORM
JEANS	LEGGINGS
SPARKLES	NO SPARKLES

Mother

this or that

— *circle your preference* —

FANCY	SIMPLE
PAINTED NAILS	NATURAL NAILS
HAIRSTYLE	NATURAL HAIR
DRESSY OUTFIT	COZY JAMMIES
DRESS SHOES	SNEAKERS
DRESS	PANTS
MAKEUP	FRESH FACE
JEWELRY	NO JEWELRY
WARM WEATHER CLOTHES	COLD WEATHER CLOTHES
BRIGHT COLORS	NEUTRALS
NO UNIFORM	SCHOOL UNIFORM
JEANS	LEGGINGS
SPARKLES	NO SPARKLES

Daughter

Dear Mom,

Daughter

List it out!

5 THINGS THAT MAKE YOU UNIQUE:

1.
2.
3.
4.
5.

Mother

List it out!

5 THINGS THAT MAKE ME UNIQUE:

1.

2.

3.

4.

5.

Daughter

ABOUT THE AUTHOR

Casey Wiegand lives in Dallas, Texas with her family. She is a mama, wife, artist, creator, and dreamer. She has been sharing her life online for years. Some of Casey's favorite things are sunshine, the color peach, her grandma's old quilts, staying in her pj's all day, pink cupcakes, and encouraging other women. The intentional home is her heart and she hopes that this journal brings intention to your relationships!

Use these tear out cards on those days she may need a little extra encouragement, Mama! Tear them out, write a heartfelt note on the back and hide it somewhere for her to find.

Mother

To know you is to love you, dear daughter. Thank you for letting me see who you truly are.

I adore you, sunshine. You are such a light!

I'll love you forever, my precious girl. Nothing could change my love for you!

Being your mama is my greatest gift!

To know you is to love you, dear daughter. Thank you for letting me see who you truly are.

I adore you, sunshine. You are such a light!

I'll love you forever, my precious girl. Nothing could change my love for you!

Being your mama is my greatest gift!

To know you is to love you, dear daughter. Thank you for letting me see who you truly are.

I adore you, sunshine. You are such a light!

I'll love you forever, my precious girl. Nothing could change my love for you!

Being your mama is my greatest gift!

To know you is to love you, dear daughter. Thank you for letting me see who you truly are.

I adore you, sunshine. You are such a light!

I'll love you forever, my precious girl. Nothing could change my love for you!

Being your mama is my greatest gift!

To know you is to love you, dear daughter. Thank you for letting me see who you truly are.

I adore you, sunshine. You are such a light!

I'll love you forever, my precious girl. Nothing could change my love for you!

Being your mama is my greatest gift!

To know you is to love you, dear daughter. Thank you for letting me see who you truly are.

I adore you, sunshine. You are such a light!

I'll love you forever, my precious girl. Nothing could change my love for you!

Being your mama is my greatest gift!